OX

D0475237

JUN   9 2011

IT'S COOL TO LEARN ABOUT COUNTRIES

Social Studies Explorer

BANGLADESH

•••• by Tamra Orr

CHERRY LAKE PUBLISHING • ANN ARBOR, MICHIGAN

Published in the United States of America
by Cherry Lake Publishing
Ann Arbor, Michigan
www.cherrylakepublishing.com

Content Adviser: Tithi Bhattacharya, PhD,
Associate Professor of History, Purdue University

Book design: The Design Lab

Photo credits: Cover and page 1, ©Ivan Stanic/Shutterstock, Inc.; cover (stamp),
©iStockphoto.com/raclro; pages 4, 13, 26, 40 and 44, ©Ryuivst/Dreamstime.
com; pages 5 and 15, ©dbimages/Alamy; page 7, ©neelsky/Shutterstock,
Inc.; page 8, ©Mark Pearson/Alamy; page 9, ©CuboImages srl/Alamy; page
10, ©Exploretimor/Dreamstime.com; page 14, ©Neil Cooper/Alamy; page 16,
©Stuwdamdorp/Alamy; page 17, ©Glyn Thomas/Alamy; page 18, ©iStockphoto.
com/ookpiks; page 20, ©andrewwheeler.com/Alamy; page 22, ©Orhan Çam/
Shutterstock, Inc.; page 22 and 38, ©Jiri Rezac/Alamy; page 28, ©Penny
Tweedie/Alamy; page 29, ©Kaikai/Dreamstime.com; page 31, ©Isa Ismail/
Shutterstock, Inc.; page 32, ©Susan Liebold/Alamy; page 33, ©Shariffc/
Dreamstime.com; page 45, ©Eye Ubiquitous/Alamy

Library of Congress Cataloging-in-Publication Data
Orr, Tamra.
    It's cool to learn about countries: Bangladesh/by Tamra Orr.
        p. cm.—(Social studies explorer)
    Includes index.
    ISBN-13: 978-1-60279-829-8 (lib. bdg)
    ISBN-10: 1-60279-829-X (lib. bdg)
    1. Bangladesh—Juvenile literature. I. Title. II. Title: Bangladesh. III. Series.
    DS393.4.O78 2011
    954.92—dc22   2009048879

Cherry Lake Publishing would like to acknowledge the work of The Partnership
for 21st Century Skills. Please visit *www.21stcenturyskills.org* for more
information.

Printed in the United States of America
Corporate Graphics Inc.
July 2010
CLFA07

TABLE OF CONTENTS

CHAPTER ONE

WELCOME TO BANGLADESH!

❖ Crowded streets are a common sight in parts of Bangladesh.

To find the country of Bangladesh on a globe or map, you need to look carefully. The entire country is slightly smaller than the state of Iowa. Still, more than 150 million people live there.

Bangladesh as a country is quite young. It did not gain independence until 1971. The culture that defines the region, however, dates back thousands of years. Poverty is a constant problem here. Even so, the history and culture of Bangladesh are rich and the country is beautiful.

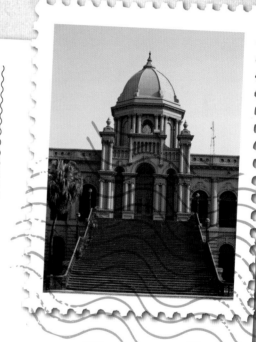

Do you like pink? If you do, you would love the Ahsan Manzil, or Pink Palace, in Dhaka. The palace was built in 1872 to house the region's nawabs, or rulers. It features 31 rooms and a huge dome. Today, the palace holds a museum. Visitors come to learn about the culture and traditions of Bangladesh.

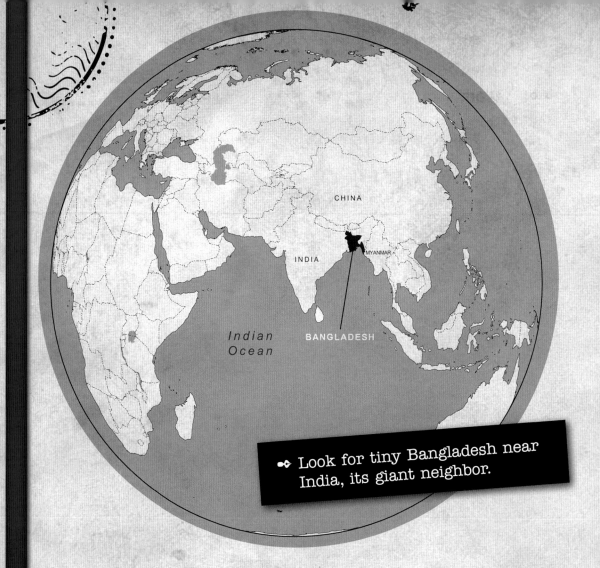

CHINA

INDIA

MYANMAR

BANGLADESH

Indian
Ocean

➤ Look for tiny Bangladesh near India, its giant neighbor.

Bangladesh is in South Asia. It measures 55,598 square miles (143,998 square kilometers).

The country has miles of flat plains of dirt and rock left behind by flood waters. Even so, most of Bangladesh is made up of water. With nearly 5,000 miles (8,000 kilometers) of rivers, lakes, swamps, and marshes, water defines the shape of the country. When the rainy season arrives, those waterways begin to swell and expand, flooding entire villages.

Southwest Bangladesh is home to more than 500 square miles (1,295 sq km) of marsh-filled forests known as the Sundarbans. The Sundarbans gets its name from the Sundari trees that take up more than half the area. Wildlife in this region is extremely diverse. Not many people live in this region. Many, however, do come here to fish. They also come to cut down trees for lumber.

Under the Sundarbans' canopy of trees walks the country's national animal: the Royal Bengal tiger. For many living in the area, this giant is literally a king of the forest. According to some beliefs, Dakshin Ray is a god who takes the form of the Royal Bengal tiger.

In the southeast of Bangladesh, the plains change to the forested mountains of the Chittagong Hill Tracts. This is home to many of the country's smaller tribes. Hatiya Island is in the Bay of Bengal off the southern coast of the country. At 25 miles (40 km) long and 9 miles (14 km) wide, it has only one road. Yet more than 300,000 people live on it. Cyclone season brings great danger to these islanders.

Victims wait for aid following a powerful cyclone that struck southwest Bangladesh in 2007.

❖ Mosques often feature beautiful geometric designs.

The capital of Bangladesh is a busy city called Dhaka. It is the largest city and home to more than 12 million people. It is also an old city, officially founded in 1608. Its history dates back even further, to the first century BCE. Throughout the years, many different beliefs have been brought to Dhaka. This is reflected in the variety of Hindu temples, Christian churches, and more than 700 Islamic **mosques** found throughout the city.

The second-largest city in Bangladesh is Chittagong. Its seaport has been known internationally since at least the 10th century. The city is also known for the nearby Shrine of Hazrat Bayazid Bostami. It includes a pond full of turtles believed to be the descendants of evil spirits. Sylhet is a city many tourists visit. It features tea gardens, waterfalls, and vast stretches of green land that turn into seas during the rainy season.

Chittagong is home to Bangladesh's main seaport.

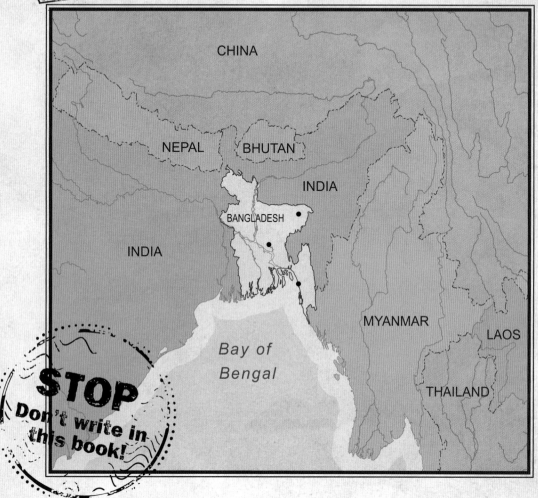

Look at this map of Bangladesh. Using a separate piece of paper, carefully trace the outline of the country. Label the cities mentioned in this chapter. Put a red circle around the capital. Look at the major rivers throughout Bangladesh. Can you see why flooding is such a problem during monsoon season and after cyclones?

Bangladesh has three seasons: winter (October to March), summer (March to June), and rainy or monsoon (June to October). Monsoons are powerful winds. In the summer, the weather is hot and humid with frequent, fast thunderstorms. Even in the winter, temperatures often pass 80 degrees Fahrenheit (27 degrees Celsius). The hottest time of year is during monsoon season, when it rains all the time. In some parts of the country, more than 235 inches (600 centimeters) of rain fall during monsoon season!

Cyclones are powerful windstorms. Through the years, a number of these storms have hit Bangladesh. Cyclones often make it difficult to find fresh drinking water.

➜ Saris are available in many colors and designs.

With such high temperatures nearly all year, keeping cool is not always easy. The key is often in wearing loose, light-colored clothing. Men usually wear loose pants or lungi. This is a long, ankle-length cloth that is wrapped around the waist. With this, they wear either a long shirt or short vest. Women typically wear loose and colorful cotton saris made from long pieces of fabric. Bangladesh is famous for jamdani saris. Jamdani cloth is made from a fine cotton material called muslin. It is then decorated with detailed designs.

CHAPTER TWO

BUSINESS AND GOVERNMENT IN BANGLADESH

↪ Police officers march in a parade celebrating Bangladesh's Independence Day.

Bangladesh's independence has been hard won. It was once the eastern part of Bengal. This region was made part of the colony of British India in the 18th century. After a long struggle, the colony gained independence in 1947. The British government divided the area into two separate states: Pakistan and India. The Bengalis living

in Bengal were separated according to religion. Western Bengal was made a part of India, a largely Hindu nation. East Bengal became East Pakistan, whose residents were mostly Muslim.

East Pakistan and West Pakistan sat on opposite sides of India, separated by a distance of approximately 1,000 miles (1,600 km). Though apparently united by a shared religion, the two parts of Pakistan came to feel separated by more than geography. Bengalis, though the majority in East Pakistan, were rarely given positions in government. They had little political power. The

➥ Dhaka's Liberation War Museum honors the difficult struggle for Bangladeshi independence.

native Bengali language and culture became more and more important to the people of East Pakistan. Declaring an independent Bengali state, separate from Pakistan, began to seem like a better and better idea.

Events reached a peak in 1971. On April 10, Bangladesh declared itself an independent nation. The Pakistani military acted against this movement. By the end of the year, at least 300,000 Bangladeshis were killed. Some claim the number to be closer to one million. The death toll was devastating. But independence was won. Sheikh Mujibur Rahman was a leader of the independence movement. In January 1972, he became the first prime minister of Bangladesh.

In the years following independence, the country has worked hard to improve its economy. Still, Bangladesh is currently one of the world's poorest nations. Nearly half of its people live below the poverty level. They struggle to make enough money for food and shelter. Many young people leave Bangladesh in search of work in nearby countries such as Singapore, Malaysia, and Saudi Arabia.

Bangladesh's currency is the Bangladeshi taka. Bills come in different amounts ranging from 1 to 500. Coins come in 1, 5, 10, 25, and 50 poishas, or cents. There are also coins for 1 and 5 taka. In 2010, one U.S. dollar was worth approximately 69.2 Bangladeshi taka.

Rice grows in many regions of Bangladesh.

More than half of the people in Bangladesh work in farming. One of the most important crops is rice. Rice is used in most meals. Another major crop is jute, a plant that is used for making rope, fishing nets, baskets, and other products. Tea is grown in the Sylhet Hills of the northeast. Wheat fields are found in the south.

ACTIVITY

The largest portion of the Bangladeshi population—63 percent—works in agriculture. Roughly 11 percent have jobs related to manufacturing and 26 percent provide services. Using these figures, create a bar graph that shows the makeup of Bangladesh's labor force. Ask an adult for help if you need it.

STOP
Don't write in this book!

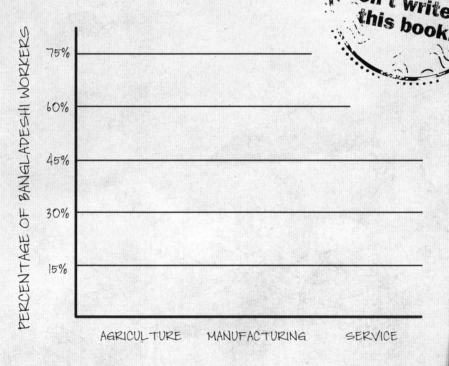

Bangladesh also produces a number of handicrafts. Jute is used to weave mats, baskets, bags, and other products. The production and use of **terra-cotta** dates back thousands of years. It has been used in cookware and other goods. Today, roofing tiles are one of the most popular uses of terra-cotta in Bangladeshi **exports**.

Not far from the capital city is the Jatiyo Smriti Soudho, or National Martyrs' Memorial. Completed in 1982, it was built to honor those who gave their lives fighting for the country's independence.

Some workers in Bangladesh make clothing. Much of the clothing is exported to other countries. This provides many jobs. But the work is often exhausting, with long hours and low pay.

Do you want to know more about Bangladesh's economy? Then take a look at its trading partners. Trading partners are the countries that **import** goods from a country or export goods to that country. Here is a graph showing the countries that are Bangladesh's top import and export trading partners.

EXPORTS ← — BANGLADESH ← — IMPORTS

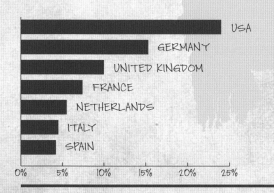

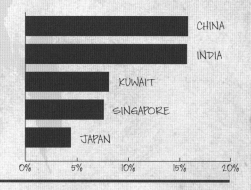

➧ Dhaka's parliament building is one example of beautiful architecture in Bangladesh.

Bangladesh has a **parliamentary** system of government. The president acts as chief of state. The prime minister holds most of the power as the head of government. President Zillur Rahman began his 5-year term in February 2009. Sheikh Hasina Wajed began her second term as prime minister the same year.

Bangladesh's government has executive, legislative, and judicial branches. Although the executive branch is headed by the president, it is the prime minister who makes most of the decisions. The legislative branch is made up of 300 people who each serve for 5 years. The judicial branch includes the Supreme Court and all of the lower courts.

The Bangladeshi flag was adopted in 1972. The background is green and represents the greenery found throughout Bangladesh. There is a bright red circle in the center. It stands for the rising sun as well as the people who sacrificed their lives to help the country gain independence.

CHAPTER THREE

A SIMPLE LIFE

❖ A boy prepares to take part in events remembering those who lost their lives for the Bangla language.

Bangladesh may be economically poor, but its culture is rich. The Bangla language is one of the most important parts of Bangladeshi identity. In fact, it is an important aspect of the country's struggle for independence. This was highlighted by the Language Movement of 1952. More than half of the population in Pakistan and nearly

all in East Pakistan spoke Bangla. Even so, Urdu had been declared the national language. On February 21, 1952, a number of university students in Dhaka were killed in a demonstration to make Bangla a state language of Pakistan.

Bangla dates back to approximately 900 BCE. It developed from the Sanskrit language. It is closely related to Hindi, which is spoken in India, and Farsi, a language used in Iran. Throughout history, Bangla has adopted vocabulary from many different languages, including English, Arabic, and Portuguese.

BANGLA

Divide a separate sheet of paper into two columns. Label one side "Vowels" and one side "Consonants." Next, using all of the letters in the English alphabet, fill out the two lists. How many letters are in each column?

In the Bangla language, there are 11 vowels and 39 consonants. What might this indicate about the language?

Virtually all of the people living in Bangladesh are Bengali. A small minority of roughly a dozen different tribal groups lives mainly in the southeast's Chittagong Hills region.

Children in Bangladesh usually spend only a short time in school before staying home to help their families. Many homes are very simple. They often consist of bamboo walls and thatched roofs with no electricity or running water. Life in the city is expensive. Those who live there often have homes made of cardboard or sheets of plastic or tin.

❧ Bamboo homes often cannot withstand powerful storm winds.

Bangla script is related to the Devanagari alphabet used for Hindi and sometimes Sanskrit. The following says "I love you" in Bangla script.

আমি তোমাকে ভালোবাসি

Most families in Bangladesh have at least four children. As children grow up and get married, the family expands to include the new members. According to tradition, multiple generations live together under the same roof. Marriages are usually arranged by the parents.

➼ Children from well-off families are the most likely to finish their schooling.

Bangladesh is traditionally a patriarchal, or male-run, society. Though legally equals, women are often given fewer opportunities in education. They are sometimes separated from men when they reach puberty. This, however, hasn't stopped women from participating in society. Bangladesh has had two female prime ministers: Khaleda Zia and Sheikh Hasina Wajed. Many women also actively fight for Bangladeshi women's rights. Taslima Nasrin is one example. Her writings have criticized unfair treatment of women. She left Bangladesh in the 1990s.

Before the 13th century, the region now called Bangladesh was mostly Hindu. Through the centuries, however, the religion of Islam spread. By the late 19th century, the majority of the region's population was Muslim. In 1988, Islam became the state religion of Bangladesh. This religion follows the Five Pillars of Islam, which include

1. making a declaration of faith;
2. praying five times each day;
3. giving to those in need;
4. fasting during the month of Ramadan;
5. making a trip to Mecca.

➥ Mecca, Saudi Arabia, is the holiest city of Islam.

A small percentage of the people in Bangladesh are Hindu. Hinduism is a religion that includes a number of gods and goddesses. Reincarnation is a central belief among Hindus. It involves the idea that a person is reborn in another body after death.

The people who live in the Chittagong Hills speak several different languages. They follow a variety of beliefs. These include **animism**, Buddhism, Christianity, and Hinduism.

Getting from place to place in Bangladesh is rarely done in a car. Very few people even own cars. With all of the flooding in the streets, boats have proven much more useful. A number of different types of boats are used to get around. Some people use canoes. Ferryboats and steamers carry larger loads, including hundreds of people. These vessels move slowly, often taking several days to reach their destinations. Some have **capsized**.

Not everyone takes to the water to get from one spot to the next. Some might grab a three-wheeled rickshaw for the trip. Nearly a quarter of a million of these brightly decorated vehicles ferry people around. Owners often cover them with images of birds, flowers, or famous actors.

➡ Do you decorate your bike? Rickshaw owners personalize their vehicles with unique decorations.

CHAPTER FOUR

LET'S HAVE FUN!

❧ Owning a color television is a sign of wealth in Bangladesh.

The people of Bangladesh know how to have fun. Some prefer joining friends to watch a cricket or football (soccer) game on someone's television. Others might spend a day in the park sipping hot tea.

In Bangladesh, the national sport is Kabaddi. It is played with two teams of 12 players each. The trick to winning is the ability to hold your breath and move quickly. The "raider" takes a deep breath. This person then touches as many of the players on the opposite team as he can. Meanwhile, he is chanting, running, and trying to not get caught, all before running out of air.

Kabaddi

Bangladesh has several historical museums, art galleries, and theaters. The Bangladesh National Museum in Dhaka has art spanning centuries, as well as a natural history department. The stages of Dhaka have produced plays that gained international acclaim, by playwrights such as Abdullah Al Mamun and Selim Al Din.

In recent years, Bangladesh has gained a reputation for excellence in the sport of chess. It has produced three International Grand Masters, including Niaz Murshed, Ziaur Rahman, and Reefat bin Sattar.

Poetry and storytelling have a long tradition of importance in Bangladesh. The 20th century poet Jasimuddin was very influential in the creation of modern Bangladeshi culture.

During festivals, actors tell folktales of mythical heroes on stage. Concerts feature instruments such as various drums, flutes, violins, and **sitars**. There are also many ways to enjoy a day without spending money, such as going to the beach or relaxing in the park.

CRAFT ACTIVITY

Concerts in Bangladesh often feature drum music. You can create your own special drum for making music.

MATERIALS:

- 2 small, clean food storage containers or stiff plastic drinking cups (it's best if each one is a different size)
- 2 balloons, 12 inches (30.5 cm) in diameter
- Scissors
- 2 medium-sized rubber bands
- 2 large rubber bands
- Paint, markers, and stickers

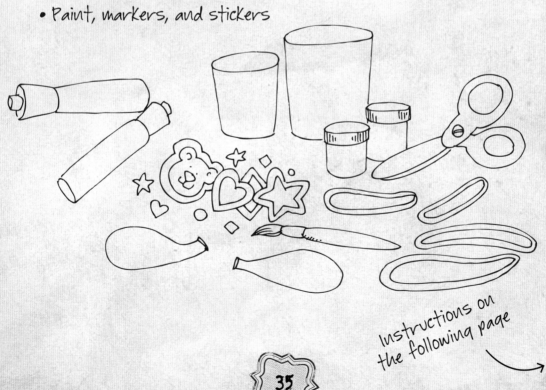

Instructions on the following page →

INSTRUCTIONS:

1. Use the scissors to cut a balloon in half across the width of the balloon. Throw away the half with the valve (the part you blow into).

2. Stretch the other half of the balloon over the open end of your drum material.

3. Pull the balloon down tight over the container or cup opening. Secure the balloon in place with a medium-sized rubber band. If possible, wrap the rubber band a second time around the container so that it is extra tight. Do not do this if you think the rubber band might snap.

4. Repeat Step #1 through Step #3 on the second container or cup.

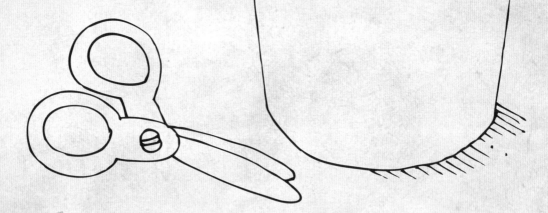

5. Place the drums next to each other. Connect them by wrapping one large rubber band around the drums, near the drumheads. Wrap the second large rubber band around the drums near the bases.

6. Decorate your drums with stickers, paint, or markers.

Play your drums with your fingers. Tap the drumheads in different spots using different amounts of pressure and try to make different sounds. Then hold the drums between your knees while sitting and make some music!

One of Bangladesh's most important holidays is Shahid Dibosh, or Martyr's Day. Shahid Dibosh is held in February. It honors those who sacrificed their lives in the fight to keep the Bangla language from being wiped out by the Pakistani government. This fight eventually inspired the Muktijuddho, the nine-month war for the country's independence in 1971. Flowers are laid at the Shaheed Minar (martyr's monument). Parties are held and people celebrate the freedom of speaking whatever language they wish. The United Nations declared this an international holiday in 1999, calling it International Mother Language Day.

• Thousands of people leave flowers at the Shaheed Minar each year.

HOLIDAYS

Here are some important holidays celebrated in Bangladesh. Many of them have to do with the country's fight for independence.

February 21	Shahid Dibosh (Martyr's Day)
Date varies	Eid-e-Milad-un-Nabi (Prophet's Birthday)
March 26	Independence Day
April 14	Bengali New Year
May 1	May Day
August 15	National Mourning Day
Date varies	Eid al-Fitr (End of Ramadan)
November 7	National Revolution Day
December 16	Bijoy Dibosh (Victory Day)
December 25	Christmas Day

CHAPTER FIVE

ON THE TABLE

Women prepare the meals in most Bangladeshi households.

When you eat a meal in Bangladesh, you can be pretty sure it will include rice. Chances are you will also drink some tea. It appears at all meals, often with sugar and milk added.

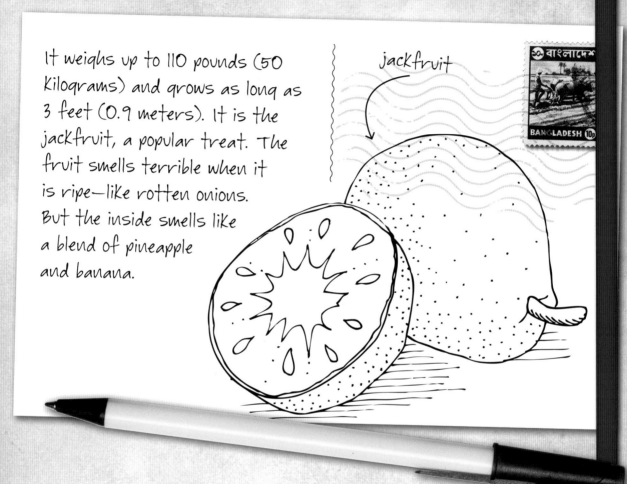

It weighs up to 110 pounds (50 kilograms) and grows as long as 3 feet (0.9 meters). It is the jackfruit, a popular treat. The fruit smells terrible when it is ripe—like rotten onions. But the inside smells like a blend of pineapple and banana.

jackfruit

Breakfast is often a light meal following morning prayers. Lunch is the largest meal of the day. It typically includes some kind of meat and rice dish, plus soup. A favorite drink is lassi. It is made from yogurt. Dinner is served late at night.

ACTIVITY RECIPE

Shemai, or sweet vermicelli, is a popular dessert in Bangladesh. This recipe involves heating ingredients on a stovetop. Be sure to have an adult help.

Shemai

INGREDIENTS
1 stick butter
2 handfuls very fine vermicelli
  (thin spaghetti noodles)
4 cups (0.9 liters) milk
1 pint (0.5 L) whipping cream
1 handful raisins
3 tablespoons (35.9 grams) sugar
4 almonds, chopped or sliced

INSTRUCTIONS

1. Have an adult melt the butter in a saucepan.
2. Break the vermicelli into pieces that are about 3 inches (7.6 cm) long.
3. Using a wooden spoon, stir the vermicelli into the butter over low heat until it turns light brown.
4. Pour in the milk and raise the heat to medium. Stir until boiling.
5. Add the raisins, almonds, and sugar.
6. Turn the stove down to low heat. Cook the mixture for another 10 minutes.
7. Add the whipping cream. Cook for another few minutes.
8. Remove the saucepan from the heat. When it is cool, chill the shemai in the refrigerator until it is time to serve.

Enjoy!

◆ Many fruits are eaten plain or used in Bangladeshi desserts.

In addition to rice, fish and other seafood from the rivers and ocean form the foundation of the Bangladeshi diet. Lamb is also very common. It is often served in the form of kabobs. Some of the dishes served in Bangladesh depend on the region. People in many cities serve daal, a dish based on a **legume** called lentils. Most dishes include at least a few dashes of garlic, ginger, cumin, cardamom, or cinnamon.

Bangladesh is a nation that faces many challenges. The proud people who call the country home have proven themselves unafraid to confront those challenges. Has the spirit of this vibrant nation inspired you to learn more, social studies explorer?

More than one-third of Bangladeshis are 14 years old or younger.

GLOSSARY

animism (AN-ih-miz-uhm) the belief that natural objects possess souls

capsized (KAP-sized) turned over or went bottom up

exports (EK-sportss) acts of selling something to another country or products sold in this way

import (IM-port) bring in from another country

legume (LEG-yoom) a plant with seeds or fruit that grow in pods, or the seeds or fruit themselves

mosques (MAHSKSS) Muslim places of worship

parliamentary (par-luh-MEN-tuh-ree) having to do with the group that has been elected to make the laws in certain countries

sitars (sih-TARZ) guitar-like instruments that are shaped like a pear with a long neck

terra-cotta (TEHR-uh KAH-tuh) a hard, fired clay that is brownish red in color

FOR MORE INFORMATION

BANGLADESH

Books

Streissguth, Tom. *Bangladesh in Pictures*. Minneapolis: VGS/ Twenty-First Century Books, 2009.

Whyte, Mariam and Yong Jui Lin. *Bangladesh*. New York: Marshall Cavendish Benchmark, 2010.

Web Sites

Central Intelligence Agency—The World Factbook: Bangladesh
www.cia.gov/library/publications/the-world-factbook/ geos/bg.html
This site offers information about Bangladesh's geography, economy, and more.

National Geographic—Bangladesh
travel.nationalgeographic.com/travel/countries/ bangladesh-guide/
Find facts and striking photos of Bangladesh.

U.S. Department of State—Bangladesh
www.state.gov/r/pa/ei/bgn/3452.htm
Read detailed data on many aspects of Bangladesh.

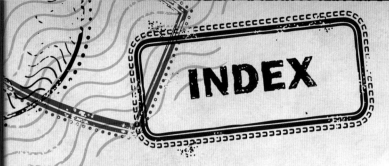

INDEX

ABOUT THE AUTHOR
Tamra Orr is the author of more than 200 books for readers of all ages. Her favorite part of writing books is learning fascinating new things about the world and its people. She and her family live in the Pacific Northwest.